How To Write a Screenplay

A Simple Building Block Process to Write a Professional Screenplay from Beginning to End!

Jennifer Chase

Also by Jennifer Chase:

Fiction:
Compulsion
Dead Game
Silent Partner

Non Fiction:
How To Write A Screenplay

http://authorjenniferchase.blogspot.com
http://jenniferchase.vpweb.com

This book is intended only to give guidance on how to write a screenplay. The advice given is for the general audience on screenwriting practices, and all contacts and agreements made with clients, publishers, agents, studios, production companies and others should be reviewed by an attorney.

JEC Press
ISBN: 978-0-982-9536-1-7

PRINTED IN THE UNITED STATES OF AMERICA

Dedicated to all aspiring screenwriters

Table of Contents

Introduction   1

Getting Started   5
   Quiz #1   8

STEP ONE: Premise & Logline   10
   Quiz #2   17
   Assignment #1   18

STEP TWO: Format   20
   Quiz #3   29
   Assignment #2   30

STEP THREE: Characters   32
   Quiz #4   39
   Assignment #3   40

STEP FOUR: Dialogue   42
   Quiz #5   48
   Assignment #4   49

STEP FIVE: Story   51
   Quiz #6   58
   Assignment #5   58

STEP SIX: Hook   60
   Quiz #7   66
   Assignment #6   67

STEP SEVEN: Set up - 1st Act   70
   Quiz #8   75
   Assignment #7   76

STEP EIGHT: Struggle & Conflict – 2ⁿᵈ Act 78
   Quiz #9 83
   Assignment #8 84

STEP NINE: Resolution – 3ʳᵈ Act 86
   Quiz #10 94
   Assignment #9 95

STEP TEN: 1ˢᵗ Draft of Screenplay 97
   Assignment #10 105

Bonus Step: Revision & Editing 107

FAQ 110

Helpful Resources & References 112

Glossary of Terms 115

Quiz Answers 119

About the Author 122

Introduction

Welcome to the wonderful and creative world of screenwriting. This is the first exciting step to writing and completing a feature length screenplay. If you purchased this book then it's likely that you already have an idea for a screenplay. If not, don't despair. This ten-step building block process is designed to get you motivated, keep you on track, and ultimately (create the first draft of your screenplay from beginning to end.) It takes the mystery out of screenwriting and gives you the most important information and step-by-step direction you need to write a professional screenplay.

I've designed this straightforward process that will give you the tools and understanding of how to write a screenplay through lessons, actual examples, self-check quizzes, and finally the building block assignments will then eventually be your first screenplay draft. Each step will build on to the next step so that you will have an actual first draft of your screenplay when you're done.

It's that easy!

I have read many books on screenwriting and have looked at the various syllabuses for screenwriting courses. I have never found one book or one class that really takes you from the beginning to end of writing a screenplay in a straightforward manner or in a short period of time. There are many books available with great information and insight to writing a screenplay, but it isn't always easy to sift through tons of information and different perspectives. It can also be frustrating and quite costly.

I have designed this book in sections of screenwriting building blocks that will walk you through the entire process of writing your screenplay.

First, you will read the lesson portion in each step as many times as necessary until you feel comfortable with the concepts.

Second, there will be an example to enhance your understanding of the lesson.

Third, you can test your comprehension of each step with a self-quiz using true/false, fill in the blank, or multiple choice questions. You will then be able to check your answers at the back of the book.

Finally, you will receive an assignment for each lesson. It will be that easy to be on your way to writing your screenplay.

The process of creating a screenplay is designed to be fun! There will be movies to watch and web site links of actual screenplays to explore and study. This book is designed to be fun, interactive and will give you results.

A screenplay is made up of action and dialogue intended to drive the story forward. Of course, along the way there's a struggle, conflict, humor, sadness, drama, and a host of other emotions and obstacles before the end. The screenwriter has the power to create and direct the characters to their final destination. Let's move forward and take a look at what's in store for your screenwriting journey.

Getting Started will get your feet wet and help you organize for what's ahead.

Premise & Logline will begin to build the foundation of your screenplay with brief outlines, plot summaries, and assistance of how "high-concept" will affect your script.

Format will jump into the format, copyright, and a glossary of terms that will take the guesswork out of the business end of screenwriting.

Characters and **Dialogue** are the fundamental building blocks that will shape your storyline and will definitely be the most fun.

Story explores the primary meaning of your script and how everything fits together.

The **Hook** is the first five to seven pages of the screenplay that grabs the reader and movie enthusiast into wanting to see more.

The **1st Act** concentrates on the setup, **2nd Act** concentrates on the confrontation and conflicts, and the **3rd Act** wraps up with the resolution of the story.

And last, but definitely not least, the conclusion concentrates on the first draft of your screenplay. You will put everything together.

These screenwriting building blocks are designed to propel you on your way to a completed professional screenplay! The more writing time you spend on each segment, the more you will benefit from this book! It will require approximately anywhere between two and four hours for each of the writing segments and sometimes more; however, it will be beneficial to spend even more time on the three act segments. You can have a completed first draft of your screenplay in as little as three months. Don't worry if you require more time on each step, it only benefits you even more. And don't' forget, you don't have to take this journey alone.

Writing should already be a part of your life in one form or another either with journal writing, short stories, poetry, or whatever most interests you. Plan ahead for the best times you will devote to writing and stick to it. By the time you finish this book, writing will have become a significant part of your life. Remember, screenwriting is just another form of expression for a writer.

What are you waiting for? Let's get started.

Getting Started

Here are some simple suggestions to help you get ready and stay organized for the duration of this book. You will be spending a considerable amount of time writing out story ideas, outlining characters, and jotting down dialogue. You don't need a specialized screenwriting program to write a screenplay, but if you already have one, that's great. If not, don't worry, you can still write a feature length screenplay using any word processor. For more information about screenwriting programs refer to the Helpful Resources & References section on page 112.

In addition to a computer with a standard word processing program, it is helpful to keep a notebook, binder, steno pad, index cards, or a composition book with you at all times to write down your ideas and to keep the screenwriting steps fresh in your mind.

These screenwriting building blocks will ultimately become the first draft of your screenplay. That is why it's very important that you have access to these ideas and outlines at all times. I always carry a small journal that has a couple of pockets with me. You can use whatever notebook works best for you.

Some writers have found it helpful to keep a writer's journal in addition to keeping a screenplay notebook. It is a place where you can write down everything you feel about your current project, future projects, schedules, or other miscellaneous ideas for the future.

I find it's helpful to keep a couple of items at my disposal. I use my laptop computer and colored index cards to shuffle characters and scenes around for my screenwriting projects. I also carry a small spiral notebook that I can tuck into my purse to jot down story notes and great character ideas that I come across throughout my day. You never know where your next inspiration for a scene or character idea will pop up.

Next, think about two or three movies that you have viewed several times and have easy access to view several times again. These movies can be current ones that you own and love or they can be new releases. As you work through each step, you will need to take time to study your favorite movie for premise, dialogue, characters, etc. It will be noted when to study a particular area of your favorite movie throughout the book. Before you know it, you'll be an expert on your favorite movies.

There will be three movies used as examples throughout the screenwriting process: **Moonstruck**, **The Sixth Sense**, and **The Matrix**. These screenplays are great examples of solid storylines and great characters.

This is also the time to begin thinking about the type of screenplay you wish to write. Determine which genre you wish to pursue. Genre refers to the type or variety of the screenplay, such as drama, horror, western, thriller, comedy, historical, mystery, action, love story, science fiction, or fantasy. And to make things more complicated there can be more specific genres, such as romantic comedy, historical drama, psychological thriller, supernatural horror, prison drama, and black comedy.

Start making screenplay notes before moving on to the next step. Write down everything that comes to mind about your first draft! This is the time where you are to prepare and brainstorm for writing your screenplay.

To summarize:

1. Keep a journal or notebook in addition to your computer writing.
2. Plan or incorporate into your daily schedule a specific time when you will be writing and try to stick to it.
3. Have at least two or three of your favorite movies you can view several times throughout the book.
4. Rent, borrow, or purchase **Moonstruck**, **The Sixth Sense**, and **The Matrix** to view several times throughout the screenwriting process.
5. Pick a genre and begin taking notes about the screenplay that you're going to write.

6. If you prefer, you can organize your writing by sections in file folders. Be sure to number each section. You can use the notes section to keep yourself organized.

Let's get started...

Quiz #1

1. **Name some form of writing material that is helpful in addition to the computer.** Index cards, Notebook, Journal

2. **What is the goal of this book?** To write a Complete Screenplay

3. **What does genre mean?** Type of Screen play (Drama)

4. **How many movies should you keep for viewing throughout this book?** 3 movies

5. **How many times should you read each step?** Several

6. **Is historical drama a genre?** Yes

7. **What is the best way to approach this class? Why?** write lots of ideas / Spend Time every day

8. **A screenplay is made up of what two elements to drive the story forward?** Premise / protestion / Plot + Act, Action + Dialogue

9. **What is the number one trait that a screenwriter must have?** Determination

10. **Name a professional screenwriter.**
Quentin Tarentino

NOTES:

ACTION + DIALOGUE - most on Screenplay.

GENRES - DRAMA, WESTERN, SciFi, Historical!

STEP ONE: Premise & Logline

The premise is the foundation or principle idea of the storyline, which will ultimately become the completed screenplay. Simply stated, this is where you begin to lay the groundwork. Don't think about the complexities at this point.

• Write down notes or the basic idea of a screenplay. The premise will most likely change as you begin to develop your story. You will begin to see what will work and what will not. Keep the brainstorming process flowing by writing out these premises in your chosen genre. Sometimes genres can overlap, like action/adventure or historical/drama. Don't worry about the overlapping or cross genres right now. Just start the process.

To begin with this step, write out basic ideas that interest you in one complete sentence. Remember, keep ideas brief, don't go into any detail yet, this is the just the brainstorming stage. You will find what works and what doesn't for your screenplay. On your computer or on 3x5 index cards, sticky notes, whatever you prefer, jot down 10-20 simple ideas that interest you.

Let me help you get started. Sometimes being a writer and getting started can be the most difficult obstacle to overcome. But once you start writing out ideas, believe me you won't be able to stop. It's like opening the floodgates to creative writing. The premise is what inspires and awakens the creativity of the screenwriter.

For example, say you're going to write a drama.

a) A man returns home two years later from the war and finds that everything has changed for him.

This is a generic sentence and doesn't offer much explanation; however, it is a basic idea or premise for a screenplay. It raises several questions. What man? What war? Is he married? Does he live in a small mid-western town or New York? Was he wounded? Is his tour of duty over?

Another example, this is actually from one of my suspense screenplays.

b) A K-9 police officer must decide to either stand by his girlfriend charged with murder or maintain the blue code of silence.

This is also a generic premise. It raises some more questions. Does this police officer know more than he's letting on? Is the department behind the murder? Is he corrupt? What does K-9 have to do with it? Did his girlfriend really murder someone? Is this a large metropolitan city police department or a small town sheriff's department?

Another example, maybe you want to write a comedy. And we need more comedies!

    c) A young, big city doctor is stranded in a small mid-western town and gets tricked into becoming the resident doctor.

Yes, this sounds familiar doesn't it? If you're thinking of "Doc Hollywood" starring Michael J. Fox, you're right! We know that he ran his classic Porsche off the road and through a fence on his way to interview for a plastic surgeon position in California. And the fence he demolished belonged to the judge in the town that sentenced him to community service as the town doctor.

But that screenplay began as a premise first. Any sound premise can eventually become a completed screenplay. If you don't remember this movie or have never seen it, I suggest you obtain a copy and review it. It's a great premise and an enjoyable movie.

Perhaps you already have an idea that you have been bouncing around for some time and that's why you purchased this book. Great! But first, keep the premise generic and brief. This is the beginning foundation for your screenplay and I want you to have a complete understanding of how screenplays are structured. It may seem a little boring, but I guarantee you will have fun soon enough giving depth to your characters and storyline. For now, hang in there.

You're probably asking what's a logline? Isn't that the same thing? Well yes and no. How's that for an answer? A logline is generally a one-line summary of the plot of the screenplay. However, with that being said, a logline can be 25 words or less describing the screenplay. A logline is still a short one line of 25 words or less that summarizes the screenplay, but it also brings in more colorful description and detail. It's an extremely important sentence. It will either pique the interest of the moviegoer, reader or producer, or not.

Let's go back to our earlier examples.

- **Premise**: A man returns home two years later from the war and finds that everything has changed for him.

Now let's look at this same sentence in more detail.

Logline: After a widowed World War II Veteran returns home to New York City, he finds himself unable to cope with the fast pace life outside of the Army.

Now we have more of a specific picture in our minds. However, it's still simple. It's actually a period piece from World War II instead of today in Iraq. This brings about a different time, perhaps a much gentler time?

Here's our second example.

Premise: A K-9 police officer must decide to either stand by his girlfriend charged with murder or maintain the blue code of silence.

Now here's a more detailed description.

Logline: When a top California K-9 cop becomes involved with an agoraphobic woman accused of murdering her sister, he finds himself caught in a web of lies and deception.

Now here are more descriptive paragraphs that help to sum up the story and logline.

When a top K-9 cop becomes involved with an agoraphobic woman accused of murdering her sister, he finds himself caught in a web of lies and deception. Can he protect her from her fears, both real and imagined before it's too late?

Jack Davis is a top K-9 cop with unprecedented integrity that finds himself falling for a beautiful suspect while struggling with departmental codes of silence.

Megan O'Connell is an agoraphobic website designer who becomes the prime suspect in the murder of her beloved sister.

Darrell Brooks, a psychopath who loves to kill, is on a quest to drive Megan insane for profit!

See the difference! We're starting to build our structure. Have fun with it!

Now here's our last example.

Premise: A young, big city doctor is stranded in a small mid-western town and gets tricked into becoming the resident doctor.

Logline: A city slicker plastic surgeon runs into trouble in a small town where he must perform community services as the resident doctor.

Be sure to take some time with story ideas of the premise and logline before continuing. Write down ideas and then work them into a basic premise and then a more detailed logline.

Moving on, I want to discuss what is meant by "high-concept". There's some debate on the actual description, but I want for you to be familiar when it is referred to in the writing of screenplays. Generally speaking, "high-concept" is an original story that has mass audience appeal – a blockbuster commercial screenplay such as The Terminator, Aliens, Heat, etc. However, movies such as Sling Blade, When Harry Met Sally, and Moonstruck are "high-concept" too.

To sum up, "high-concept" is a specific, original screenplay with mass audience appeal that can be summed up in one to three sentences. By industry standards, not all screenplays are considered "high-concept" with mass audience appeal. Take for example, small independent films or films appealing to smaller audiences such as some foreign movies and the so-called "chic flicks".

There have been quite a few things to digest in this second step. Take your time and re-read this section as often as necessary. Write down in your own words definitions for high-concept, premise, and logline in your notebook or on 3x5 cards so you can refer to them as often as needed. Write down all of your ideas at this point. This step is to help you get started and to motivate you to write a completed screenplay.

Remember, have fun with all of your story ideas and make sure you have fully understood the concepts before moving on to the next step. Take the self-check quiz and then you will be ready to begin your first assignment in the building block steps of screenwriting.

Quiz 2:

1. **Which of the following is a screenplay genre.**
   a. war historical
   b. action adventure
   c. black comedy
   d. all of the above
   e. none of the above

2. _High Concept_ **is a detailed original idea of the screenplay that has mass audience appeal.**

3. _Premise_ **is the principle idea of a screenplay.**

4. _Logline_ **is one line summary of the screenplay.**

5. **A logline is still a short one line of 25 words or less that summarizes the screenplay because it brings a more colorful description and detail to the idea.** True or False?

6. **A K-9 police officer must decide to either stand by his girlfriend charged with murder or maintain the blue code of silence.**
   a. high-concept
   b. premise
   c. logline
   d. both a and b
   e. both a and c

7. **A city slicker plastic surgeon runs into trouble in a small town where he must perform community services as the resident doctor.**
   a. high-concept
   b. premise
   c. logline
   d. both a and b
   e. both a and c

8. **Which movie is considered "high concept"?**
   a. Romancing the Stone
   b. Psycho
   c. City Slickers
   d. The Borne Identity
   e. None of the above

f. All of the above

9. **All screenplays need to fall under the screenplay heading of "high concept".** True or False?

10. **Premise is the imaginative way for a screenwriter to brainstorm with basic ideas of the screenplay.** True or False?

Assignment #1:

✓ **Write 3 original loglines of your own.**

✓ **Write 3-5 descriptive sentences for each original logline.**

✓ **Write 2 loglines from any of your favorite movies.**

✓ **Feel free to write as many loglines and descriptions as you can. This will only further develop your understanding of the beginning stages of screenwriting and help to finalize your idea for your screenplay.**

NOTES:

STEP TWO: Format

I like to get the business screenplay aspects out of the way early. This step addresses the business aspect and actual structure of a screenplay. We're getting down to the nitty-gritty of screenwriting essentials. It's the where, when, and why to copyright? What does some of the screenplay jargon really mean? And, how do you properly format your screenplay?

Read this step carefully and refer to the information as a reference throughout your class screenwriting experience. Be sure to visit the websites noted and save as your favorite places on your computer.

COPYRIGHT

First, it's extremely important to copyright any screenplay. Why? It protects the written works and the writer as a legal proof of originality from fraud and theft. A screenwriter copyrights the screenplay before it's sent out to anyone, namely agents, production companies, or script consultants.   This is done after several re-writes and the screenwriter feels that the script is polished and ready to go.

Library of Congress
Copyright Office
101 Independence Avenue SE
Washington, DC 20559-6000
(202) 707-3000

Send all of the following to the above Library of Congress address or you can copyright by using their online features (See below).

1.   Complete and sign an application on <u>Form PA</u>

2.   Submit a complete copy of the original screenplay

3.   A check, money order, or bank draft payable to Register of Copyrights in the amount of $45.00 ($35.00 online)

4.   Send out complete packet with a return receipt request

For more complete information go to the copyright website:

<u>http://www.copyright.gov/</u>

Second, many screenwriters have found it to be extremely useful to register their screenplay through the Writers Guild of America – West. This form of registering your screenplay is <u>NOT</u> to be in place of copyrighting through the Library of Congress./ This form of registering is intended to register your screenplay as legal evidence and establishes a date for the material's existence./ Writers Guild of America – West is a neutral, third party that can establish evidence and the actual date of the screenplay.

WGA – West Registry
7000 West Third Street
Los Angeles, CA 90048
(323) 782-4500

Registration Fees - $20.00 for general public and $10.00 for WGA members in good standing. The screenplay and payment can be mailed or hand delivered to the above address.

For more complete information regarding Writer's Guild of American – West Registry go to the website:

http://www.wgawregistry.org/webrss/

GLOSSARY OF SCREENWRITING TERMS

Let's first take a look at some common screenplay terminology. It's important to understand terms and directions in reading and writing a screenplay. Throughout this book, you'll be asked to read several scripts in reference to the Step you're studying. The following list will help you to understand not only what the screenplay is referring to, but understand industry terminology.

Action
The scene description, character movement, and sound described in a screenplay.

Beat
It refers to an interruption in dialogue. It suggests that the character (actor) should pause a moment before continuing the dialogue.

b.g. (background)
This term is used to describe an action in the background when the attention is focused on the foreground.

(RICK BLAIR) - CASABLANCA.

Character
The name of the character appears in ALL CAPS when the character is first introduced in the "Action". The character is then written in normal letters in the action and the rest of screenplay.

CLOSE ON
It refers to a camera shot description that suggests a close-up on a person, action, or object.

CONTINUOUS
It refers to an action that moves from one location to another without interruptions of time.

Coverage
This refers to the 3-5 page report that evaluates the potential of a screenplay. This report will recommend, consider, or pass on the screenplay project.

Copyright
This process protects the written works and the writer as legal proof of originality from fraud and theft. (See copyright information above in Step 2: Format)

Cross-Genre
Refers to two mixed genres (see genre). For example, action/adventure, historical/drama, and horror/comedy are cross-genres.

CUT TO:
This refers to a simple transition of scene, character changes, or frame change.

Development
This is the process when a screenplay is developed into a shooting script.

Dialogue
This refers to what characters say in the screenplay.

Direction
This refers to the description of the action in a screenplay.

DISSOLVE TO:
Another common transition, when one scene fades out and another comes into view – also see FADE TO:

EXT.
This simply means exterior. This particular scene takes place outdoors.

FADE TO:
See DISSOLVE TO:

FADE IN:
This refers to the beginning of a screenplay.

FADE OUT.
This refers to the end of the screenplay.

Genre
Refers to the type or variety of the screenplay. For example, comedy, sci-fi, action, and drama are a type of genre.

High-Concept
This refers to an original story that has mass audience appeal. For example, high-concept is a blockbuster commercial screenplay.

Hook
This refers to an incident or happening that makes the audience interested in the movie.

INSERT
This refers to a close-up of an important detail in the screenplay.

INT.
This simply means interior. This particular scene takes place indoors.

Logline
This refers to a one-line summary of the plot and can be 25 words or less describing the screenplay.

Option
This refers to a producer who pays for the rights of the screenplay in a specified period of time.

O.S. (off screen)
This refers to a character's dialogue heard and not seen on the screen.

Personal Direction
This refers to the character's specific direction. For example, sighing, laughing, or yelling are personal directions.

POV
This simply means point of view. It is where we see through someone else's eyes.

Premise
This refers to the foundation or principle idea of the storyline.

Query Letter
This refers to a short letter pitching a professional company in hopes that they will request to read your screenplay.

Scene
This refers to an event that takes place in one location or time.

Spec Script
This refers to a written screenplay that is intended to be sold on the open market but not by a studio or production company. The only way for a new screenwriter to break into the business is to have a strong spec script.

Treatment

This refers to the plot of a screenplay written in one to two pages. The treatment should include the entire well-written story with a beginning, middle, and end.

V.O. (voice over)
This refers to a character's voice heard either prior to seeing them or as a narration of a specific event.

SCREENPLAY FORMAT

There is a definite physical format to screenwriting. As mentioned previously, a screenplay is made up of action and dialogue. Sounds easy enough? Not entirely, but absolutely attainable with training along with the will to succeed. If you don't have specialized screenwriting software, here are some guidelines to help get you started in a standard word processing program. Some specialized programs may be slightly different in margin settings, but this will help you to get started.

Format tips for getting started:

1. All of these tab settings can be stored in a Macro
2. Turn off justification
3. Create a Header for page numbers that will carry to each page (except page 1)
4. Top and Bottom Margins need to be set to ½ inch (.50")
5. Left Margin 1 inch (1.00")
6. Right Margin ¾ inch (.75")
7. Set Tab Settings:

1"	Margin
1.6"	Direction
2.6"	Dialogue
3.3"	Personal Direction
3.9"	Character Name
5.9"	Transitions
7.2"	Page #

8. Courier 12-point font.

9. 8 ½ x 11 regular white paper

Here's an example from my screenplay "Silent Partner" from page one.

```
                    "SILENT PARTNER"



FADE IN:

EXT. STREETS (1:25AM) - NIGHT

        A Sheriff's Deputy patrols the quiet streets in
        the heart of a small California coastal town,
        slowing the police cruiser only when there are
        quick FLASHES of light in the shadows as a few
        transients enjoy their scrounged cigarette butts
        and booze.

INT. POLICE CRUISER - NIGHT

        OFFICER JACK DAVIS (35) with dark hair and
        intense blue eyes surveys the dark corners of the
        streets, casually running his fingertips through
        his military haircut.

                            JACK
                You're such an adrenaline junkie.  The
                end doesn't justify the means.
                        (sighs)
                I can't even look at you right now.
                You have to start following
                procedures.  Just because you sleep
                with me doesn't make this any easier.
```

```
                      (beat)
          Do you have anything to say?
```

Take a moment to study the new terms in the screenplay. Look at the title in ALL CAPS with quotes. Look at FADE IN: and where it's located. It begins with EXT. – an outside location - the streets at night. It then gives up the action of the patrol car on the city streets. Then the scene is INT. – an interior location of the police cruiser. We are then introduced to our character - Jack.

There are quite a few things to digest in this step. Take your time and carefully study everything several times and test your knowledge by taking the self-check quiz.

Now that the business side of screenwriting is done, we're going to have some fun creating our characters and dialogue in the next two steps!

Quiz 3:

1. **When should you copyright your screenplay?**
   a. When you have finished your screenplay
   b. Before you finish your screenplay
   c. When you've polished your script and before you send it to an agent, production company, or script consultant
   d. Only if you send it to a production company
   e. None of the Above

2. **When does "Development" affect a screenplay?**
   a. When you've got the premise for a screenplay
   b. When a production company develops the screenplay into a shooting script
   c. When a simple transition changes into another transition
   d. When you write a query letter
   e. None of the Above

3. **Where should you send your screenplay for copyrighting?**
   a. Writers Guild of America – West Registry
   b. Production Company
   c. Agent
   d. Library of Congress
   e. None of the Above

4. **What is "Action" referred to in a screenplay?**
   a. The scene description, character movement, or sounds described in a screenplay
   b. The 3-5 page report that evaluates the potential of a screenplay
   c. The camera shot description that suggests a close-up on a person, action, or object.
   d. The outdoor scene
   e. None of the Above

5. **What should the top and bottom margins be set at for your screenplay?**
   a. ¼ inch
   b. ½ inch
   c. ¾ inch
   d. 1 inch
   e. None of the Above

6. **You should have the justification turned off for your screenplay format.**

True or False?

7. **Option refers to a producer who pays for the rights of the screenplay in a specified period of time.**
   True or False?

8. **EXT. refers to the interior scene in the screenplay.**
   True or False?

9. **Premise and Logline are the same thing.**
   True or False?

10. **Why should you register your screenplay with the Writer's Guild of America – West?**
    a. It's better than copyrighting
    b. They are a neutral, third party that can establish evidence and the date of the screenplay.
    c. They are part of the process when a screenplay is developed into a shooting script.
    d. They have mass audience appeal.
    e. None of the Above

Assignment #2:

✓ **Finalize your logline. By this time you should have a good idea of the screenplay you're going to write. If not, take some time and review the previous steps and only continue when you have a firm grasp of premise and logline.**

✓ **Write a minimum of 2-3 paragraphs for each the protagonist and the nemesis of your original screenplay. Describe each character in detail. Have some fun with this section. Don't worry about writing too much.**

✓ **Keep brainstorming and writing down everything that comes to mind about your screenplay.**

NOTES:

STEP THREE: Characters

Creating believable characters is essential in the screenwriting process. If the audience doesn't struggle with your characters, then the storyline won't matter no matter how great the screenplay premise. In other words, interesting characters that make us laugh, cry, hate, and love are what make up great characters. We want to see them succeed, conquer or become enlightened in some way. The character could start out as mean and insensitive in the beginning and end up loving and caring in the end. Or, a character could be shy and timid and through their triumphs become confident and assertive. Changes to a character throughout the screenplay doesn't have to be so bold like black and white, they can go through subtle changes. The bottom line, a character must change in some way. That's why it's so important to know your characters inside and out.

Now, let's define protagonist. The protagonist is the central character or "hero" in the screenplay. This character is extremely important in that he or she drives the story plot forward. And throughout the screenplay, the protagonist must endure conflicts and stumbling blocks in order to reach their goal. Through conflicts they must reassess on how they are going to get what they want. They must change in some way based on what they encounter.

There is only one protagonist in a screenplay. That's not to say that there aren't other characters that help the protagonist; for example, a mentor, sidekick, neighbor, mother, sister, cousin, love interest, or family friend. We'll refer to these characters as supporting characters. These characters are important to the protagonist as well as to the storyline.

Now, let's define nemesis. The nemesis, or antagonist, is sometimes referred to as the "villain" and has a particular interest in defeating the protagonist. Most of the time the nemesis is of particular interest to the hero. Keep in mind that the protagonist and nemesis aren't always like the "good guys" and "bad guys" in a comic hero movie or blasting action movie. They can be more subtle characters, such as a father and son or a boss and employee. Sometimes the nemesis is something that we can't see, like a fear, natural disaster, or a ghost.

Let's take some examples from three completely different screenplays that I've chosen to illustrate. Feel free to acquire these movies for the duration of the book.

1.   Screenplay: <u>The Matrix</u>

Protagonist: Neo

Nemesis: Agent Smith

Supporting: Trinity & Morpheus

2.   Screenplay: <u>Moonstruck</u>

        Protagonist: Loretta

        Nemesis: Mr. Johnny & Ronny

        Supporting: Cosmo & Rose

3.   Screenplay: <u>The Sixth Sense</u>

        Protagonist: Malcolm

        Nemesis: The Dead

        Supporting: Cole & Lynn

Now, let's look primarily at the protagonists and how they are introduced in each of the screenplays.

Neo from "The Matrix" is described as "a younger man who knows more about living inside a computer than living outside one". What does this tell you about him? It makes us think that he's some kind of computer genius and that he lives only for the computer. He probably doesn't have many friends or social life. Maybe his life outside the computer is a complete mess because of his past experiences and he drowns himself inside the workings of the computer. His description leaves more to the

imagination and is developed through his
actions and dialogue throughout the screenplay.

Loretta from "Moonstruck" is simply described
with more physical details as "Italian, 37. Her
hair black, done in a dated style, is flecked
with grey. She's dressed in sensible but
unfashionable clothes of a dark color". We
immediately get a clear physical picture of our
protagonist. But what are her feelings, beliefs,
and dreams? Again, we learn more about her
character through her actions and dialogue
through out the screenplay.

These two completely different character examples give us great
introductions to the protagonists in the screenplays. The screenwriters
have developed these characters, but through dialogue and action we
learn more about these characters as the plot moves along.

The last character example, Malcolm from
"The Sixth Sense" is introduced as "in his
thirties with thick, wavy hair and striking,
intelligent eyes that squint from years of
intense study. His charming, easy-going smile
spreads across his face". We get the

impression that he's kind and loving. Good at
his job from studying so much, someone with
higher education like a doctor or lawyer.

What's interesting about these three particular screenplays is that they differ with the protagonist and nemesis. "The Matrix" is the typical screenplay storyline of good versus evil. "Moonstruck" has a relationship conflict between the two main characters. And last, "The Sixth Sense" has an unusual relationship between the protagonist and nemesis, in the fact that the nemesis is something that we basically can't see. Think about how these characters are worked into the screenplay storyline.

Now, take your premise and logline of the screenplay that you're going to write and create your protagonist. Here are some things to think about when you are creating your characters. Make them "real". Believe that your characters are real people. Think of every possible characteristic and attribute. The more realistic the characters are the better the screenplay. How do they think? What sets them off? What makes them laugh? What happened to them as a child? Think about their internal and external conflicts.

Here's a list of 25 things that will help you to begin creating your protagonist. Start by examining this initial list and keep working with your character in detail.

View your 2 or 3 favorite movies for inspiration. Have fun with this! You can create any type of character. The possibilities are endless! You must love ALL of your characters if you want to develop rich and believable characters in your screenplay.

1. Name

2. Nick name

3. Physical Characteristics

4. Age

5. Sex

6. Married/Single?

7. Beliefs/Religion

8. Family

9. Friends

10. Occupation

11. Work habits

12. Unemployed?

13. Rent/Own House

14. Favorite food/drink

15. Favorite car

16. Exercise?

17. Pets?

18. Favorite hang out

19. Education

20. Fears/Dislikes?

21. Hang ups/Bad habits

22. Shy/Outgoing?

23. Intelligent/Under achiever?

24. Goals

25. *Internal/External Conflicts

For more inspiration, view some of the scripts located at:

http://www.simplyscripts.com/movie.html

Work with your protagonist until you know exactly how he/she thinks, talks, and reacts under <u>any</u> condition. Work with your nemesis and supporting characters as well. Know ALL your characters inside and out. I can't stress this simple fact enough.

In the next step you will be creating dialogue for your characters that will bring them to life. Take your time with this important step and don't rush. It will <u>set the tone</u> for the rest of the screenplay.

Quiz #4:

1. **Which one of the following is NOT a characteristic for a protagonist?**
    a.   hair color
    b.   occupation
    c.   religious beliefs
    d.   favorite car
    e.   None of the Above

2. **Creating believable characters in a screenplay is essential.**
    True or False?

3. **The protagonist and nemesis are the same person.**
    True or False?

4. **The protagonist rarely interacts with the nemesis.**
    True or False?

5. **The protagonist is sometimes referred to as the hero in the screenplay.**
    True or False?

6. **When we are introduced to the character Loretta in "Moonstruck", which characteristic is NOT introduced by the screenwriter?**
    a.   Italian, 37
    b.   long wavy hair
    c.   dressed in sensible clothes
    d.   black hair
    e.   All of the Above

7. **The name and physical description of the protagonist are the most important characteristics for that character in a screenplay.** True or False?

8. **What is a protagonist?**
    a. The most understanding character in the screenplay.
    b. The most interesting character in the screenplay.
    c. The central character in the screenplay.
    d. The villain character in the screenplay.
    e. None of the Above

9. **Creating believable characters that the audience can identify with is important.** True or False?

10. **When should you create a profile for your characters in the screenplay?**
    a. Before you begin writing the screenplay.
    b. After you're finished writing the screenplay.
    c. After you have a solid premise to the screenplay.
    d. Only when you have a title for the screenplay.
    e. None of the above

Assignment #3:

View one of your favorite movies, preferably a couple of times. Take one scene from the movie where there is dialogue between two characters. The scene can be one to three minutes long.

✓ **Write down the dialogue between the two characters. Read this dialogue several times. I guarantee you won't look at movies the same way.**

✓ **Write a brief explanation of how the dialogue was created for these particular characters and try to get into each character's head. What were they thinking? Why did they act in a certain way? What do they hope to get out of the conversation?**

✓ **Now, write a scene between two of your characters. It doesn't matter if you use this scene for your screenplay or not. Get into the habit of creating dialogue for your characters. Spend some time with this step; it will only help to enhance your screenwriting process.**

✓ **You should be writing on a regular basis and using your notebooks or journals to assist you.**

NOTES:

STEP FOUR: Dialogue

Congratulations! You're making great progress. Hopefully you're having fun with this screenplay process. Before you know it you'll have a complete professional screenplay in front of you.

Let's quickly review. By now you should have a writing schedule that works for you. Pay attention to what goes on around you in your daily activities. It's a great time to observe situations and people. It will give you some inspiration if you're feeling a bit overwhelmed or suffering from writer's block. Don't forget to jot things down in your notebook or in whatever form you've chosen.

We've learned about premise, log lines, and correct screenplay format. And now you should have a good understanding of your characters. Hopefully, you've taken the time and read a few screenplays and have viewed your favorite movies with some new insight. All you need now is great dialogue to introduce your characters and move the audience through the journey of the screenplay.

Dialogue sounds easy enough. And it can be. But keep in mind that one full page of a screenplay is approximately equal to one minute of screen time. With that being said, it's important for a screenplay not to have any unnecessary dialogue. In other words, you want to make sure that the dialogue is just enough to tell the story and move it along at an engaging pace. Here are a few tips to remember when writing dialogue.

> ➢ Keep dialogue to short sentences in order to not bog down the flow of information and the storyline.

> ➢ Dialogue must be like "real life" conversations and not perfectly punctuated English.

> ➢ Stay away from lengthy monologues unless it's <u>absolutely</u> necessary for the scene and storyline (i.e. resolution moment, major character realization, turning point etc.).

> ➢ Stay true to each of the individual character's dialogue.

> ➢ Don't explain everything that's going on in the screenplay (save what you can for action, it's a "show don't tell" screenplay theory).

Listen to conversations in your everyday life. People don't speak perfect English and some speak more slang than proper English. It will depend on your specific character.

For example:

```
                              BOB
                Hey dude, what's up?

                              RICK
                Nothing.  Just been chillin.  Vanessa
                has been hassling me about my work.
                              (sighs)
                I can't get anything right.
```

Now take a look at the same conversation, but with different dialogue.

```
                              BOB
                Good morning Rick.  How have you been?

                              RICK
                I've been okay - thanks.  Vanessa gave
                me a poor work evaluation on Friday.
                              (sighs)
                She's never going to see all the hard
                work I do around here.
```

What can be said about Bob and Rick? The first set of dialogue we can assume that they are young buddies with slang dialogue. Maybe surfing buddies? Or, old high school chums?

The second set of dialogue is a bit more formal. Maybe they are a couple of guys who work for a corporation of some type – like a software company.

See the difference in dialogue and how it can affect the tone of your story? You want to make sure that the conversations reflect how that particular character speaks. A bank president wouldn't say, "hey dude" and a skateboard champion probably wouldn't say, "I was completely engrossed with that Walt Whitman poem you gave me."

If you observe and listen to everyday conversations, most people don't speak in complete, grammatically correct sentences.

For example:

```
                              BOB
          Hey?   What's up?

                              RICK
          Not much.   Was out at the beach.
          Totally cool waves.
```

This dialogue demonstrates the light banter between buddies. Keep all of this in mind when you're writing dialogue for your characters.

Here's an example of a scene with dialogue of a woman trying to get out of a speeding ticket (from my actual screenplay "Housewife Syndrome").

```
EXT. ALLEY'S CAR - MORNING

Alley eases the car to the side of the street
under an overgrown shade tree.

OFFICER BUCK slowly walks with authority toward
the vehicle.  He is a large, middle-aged man with
very developed muscles.

Alley examines her side mirror closely as the
policeman approaches her car.  She has a big
smile on her face.

                         ALLEY
          Hi Officer. Did I do something wrong?

                         OFFICER BUCK
                    (leaning over to the window)
          Ma'am did you happen to see how fast
          you were going?

                         ALLEY
                    (glancing back at the girls)
          Why didn't I tell you girls that my
          speedometer seemed to be acting kinda
          funny?
                    (to officer)
          Because I try to be extremely careful
          when driving in residential areas.
          Especially
```

with children and dogs.

All ladies nod in agreement.

> OFFICER BUCK
> You didn't notice that you were
> driving twenty miles an hour over the
> speed limit?

> ALLEY
> Well it's just that you can't be too
> careful these days. Am I right?

> POLICEMAN BUCK
> Yes of course, but you...

> ALLEY
> It's just that four little ol' girls
> such as ourselves could fall prey to
> unscrupulous criminals.

> OFFICER BUCK
> (softening)
> It's true ma'am. It's a wonder what
> the world is coming to.

> ALLEY
> (smiling)
> We just saw a whole special on those
> terrible car-jackings and how they
> prey upon just average housewives.

> OFFICER BUCK
> It's true. We've had three just in
> the last two weeks.

> ALLEY
> I feel so vulnerable. What can I do
> to protect myself? Could you help
> us?

The Officer straightens his belt and casually
looks around the neighborhood.

All four ladies watch him with curiosity.

> OFFICER BUCK
> (smiling)
> We are not suppose to tell civilians
> this- But... you ladies should know
> how to handle firearms.

> ALLEY
> (acting surprised)

```
                           Do  you  really  think  that  I  could
                           handle  one  of  those  nasty  looking
                           guns?

                                     OFFICER BUCK
                           No doubt in my mind ma'am.

     The Officer WRITES something down on his
     notebook.

                                     ALLEY
                                   (frowning)
                           Are  you  giving  me  a  ticket?

     The Officer hands Alley a piece of paper.

                                     OFFICER BUCK
                           My  shift  ends  in  two  hours.   If
                           you're  interested,  meet  me  at  this
                           address  and  I'd  be  happy  to  show  you,
                           all  of  you  how  to  shoot.   A  few  of  us
                           guys  have  a  shooting  range  up  in  the
                           hills  to  help  us  relax.

                                     ALLEY
                                   (smiling)
                           We'll  be  there.
```

Get familiar with writing quick dialogue for your characters. Look to your favorite movies and everyday life for inspiration. Study the dialogue! You'll be amazed by how much you'll learn about dialogue and character development by your surroundings.

Be extremely familiar with all of your characters, even if your character just has a bit part. Have fun because you're beginning to breathe life into your characters and into your screenplay.

Before moving on, be very comfortable with your characters and dialogue. The next step will dig deep into the story of your screenplay. Remember write… write… and write some more.

Quiz #5

1. **Strong dialogue should have the following:**
    a.   short quick sentences
    b.   long monologues
    c.   plenty of slang
    d.   complete grammatically correct sentences
    e.   none of the above

2. **When should you have monologues in your screenplay?**
    a.   never
    b.   sometimes
    c.   always
    d.   when absolutely necessary
    e.   none of the above

3. **You should always stay true to your character's dialogue.**
    True or False?

4. **Your character should always speak correct English instead of slang.**
    True or False?

5. **Always explain through your character's dialogue what is going on in your screenplay.**
    True or False?

6. **Which guideline is <u>NOT</u> helpful when writing dialogue.**
    a. stay true to your character's dialogue
    b. keep sentences short and to the point
    c. use action to "show don't tell" instead of dialogue
    d. use monologues only when necessary
    e. none of the above

7. **You can find inspiration for writing dialogue at the following places.**
    a. Mall
    b. grocery store
    c. company party
    d. gym
    e. none of the above
    f. all of the above

8. **Dialogue is only limited by the screenwriter.**
    True or False?

9. **When creating dialogue always keep within the boundaries of the specific character.**
    True or False?

10. **Never create dialogue for minor characters the same way as for the major characters.**
    True or False?

Assignment #4:

✓ **Write a brief outline (3 – 6 paragraphs or more for each act) of your story with beginning, middle, and end of your screenplay. Take the time to really think about your story. This is an important step. You will be revising and further developing the story and acts as time goes on.**

✓ **Write a list of things that you will need to research and how you will be conducting research. It's never too early to begin to think about research.**

NOTES:

STEP FIVE: Story

This next step is an essential building block for your screenplay. It is the glue that holds the rest of your screenplay building blocks together. Up to this point, you have learned about premise, log line, screenplay format, constructing characters, and writing dialogue to bring all of your characters to life. Now you must string together scenes that will become your acts, which in turn will be the story of your screenplay.

What is story? The easiest way to define story is to call it the "main event" of the screenplay. It is the series of scenes and acts that builds to one major event. This event takes the protagonist from beginning to end. Along the way, the protagonist goes through a series of conflicts to a final resolution. There must be some kind of change from the beginning point of the screenplay to the final ending. It must be an absolute and permanent change.

Remember, one page of a screenplay is approximately one minute of screen time. An average screenplay is anywhere from 90 to 120 pages or 1 ½ to 2 hours. Of course, there are always exceptions with long epic movies or short subject films. For the most part, keep your written screenplay on track with no more than 120 pages. If possible, you should have 95 to 110 pages of a tightly written screenplay.

What is a screenplay really?

Now lets break down exactly how a story is constructed.

- ➢ Action and Dialogue = Scenes
- ➢ Scenes = Acts
- ➢ Acts = Beginning + Middle + End
- ➢ Beginning + Middle + End = Story
  - ✓ Story Beginning = 1st Act (set up)
  - ✓ Story Middle = 2nd Act (struggle & conflict)
  - ✓ Story End = 3rd Act (resolution)

It's important to understand how a screenplay is constructed. It's not a simple formula, but rather a "writing form", which enables you to have creative control over your story. The above illustration is a simple screenplay breakdown that will enable you to create a process that transfers from paper to screenplay form. Remember, a screenplay differs from all other writing forms in that it is only action and dialogue.

In review, action refers to the description or narrative of what's happening in the scene. Dialogue is the conversation between characters. The action and dialogue make up a scene. The scene or the "story event" is notated by INT. or EXT. at the beginning of each scene. Every scene needs to have some change. If the scene remains unchanged by the end, then it's meaningless. Make sure every scene has some sort of exchange in the character's life. It doesn't have to be a major life changing event, but some type of change. Every scene must possess an action then reaction to keep the story moving forward. Scenes make up the Acts that result in the 3 Acts (beginning, middle, end) of your screenplay.

Simply stated, the 1st Act is the beginning of your story. The story beginning is the "setup" to the rest of your screenplay. This is an extremely important element. Without a strong beginning, the rest of the screenplay will fall short. Don't rush your screenplay without taking the time to properly set it up.

The story middle is the 2nd Act, or the body of the screenplay where all of the protagonist's struggles and conflicts occur. This is where you take audiences on a journey of adventure. Anything is possible. There should be some type of consequence to the protagonist in decisions he/she makes.

The 3rd Act is the final wrap-up or resolution to the screenplay. This the shortest act of the screenplay and it finalizes the story. Will the protagonist get what he/she wants? Will the worst thing happen? Or, the best?

Remember to organize your story with a beginning, middle, and end. Scrutinize every scene in order to convey the feelings and desires of your characters.

RESEARCH

I want to talk a little bit about research that adds realism to your screenplay. With every screenplay you write, there will be a certain amount of research involved. Sometimes just a little bit of investigation and other times you will have a considerable amount of study on a subject.

For example, a small amount of background is necessary if you are writing about a protagonist that is a marine scientist, master gardener, veterinarian, or police officer. More time and examination is necessary if you're writing a historical screenplay based on the Civil War or life and times in the 1920s.

Make research an important part of your screenwriting process. Use several resources when conducting research.

- ✓ Library
- ✓ Internet
- ✓ Newspapers
- ✓ Magazines
- ✓ Bookstores (even used bookstores)
- ✓ Movies/Videos
- ✓ Informational Television
- ✓ Professional Institutions
- ✓ Interviews
- ✓ Professionals in related fields
- ✓ Friends
- ✓ Family
- ✓ Neighbors
- ✓ Local Businesses

Here are four important things to remember about conducting research.

1. Don't limit yourself to one or two resources.

2. There's no such thing as too much research.

3. Know your subject well before you begin writing about it.

4. Make sure your research is important to your story.

Research is a wonderful tool because it gives your story and characters depth. Your screenplay will result in a rich and well-developed storyline.

TITLE

A title for your screenplay is also a very important factor. Sometimes you have a title right out of the gate and other times you can be almost finished writing your screenplay before a title seems to fit.

Take your time and don't rush your title. I find it easier to have a page in a notebook with several titles that I add to or eliminate. You'll be amazed going through the screenwriting process how your decisions change on what's the best title. Look at movie titles too; this will help to stimulate the creative process of titling your screenplay. There are quite a few titles out there to help inspire you. A general rule is that most titles are short and to the point with one or very few words. Be creative. Good luck!

TITLE PAGE

Last, I wanted to touch on the title page of your script. Once you have a title, your title page should look something like this:

"GREAT TITLE"

by

John Smith

123 1st Street
Los Angeles, CA 97632
(213) 555-1122

Be sure to go to the web links with completed screenplays to help you become familiar with screenplays and how they are constructed.

Work on your story and have a firm grasp on the beginning, middle, and end. Take your time. This is a good time to review everything up to this step before moving forward. You should have outlines of your characters and your complete story. Work with these outlines until you feel that you know your story and characters from every angle.

You are in control of your screenwriting story! Get creative and enjoy the screenwriting process!

Quiz #6

1.   **What makes up a scene?**

2.   **What is story?**

3.   **What is action?**

4.   **What is dialogue?**

5.   **One page of a screenplay is how long in movie time?**

6.   **What is an act?**

7.   **How many acts are in a screenplay?**

8.   **Explain the 1st act in a screenplay?**

9.   **Explain the 2nd act in a screenplay?**

10.   **Explain the 3rd act in a screenplay?**

Assignment #5:

✓ **Review what you wrote about in your brief outline for the beginning, middle, and end of your screenplay. Update it often.**

✓ **Write a paragraph describing your hook and how your beginning scenes will set it up.**

✓ **Think about your research and makes notes.**

✓ **Think about what you might want to title your screenplay and jot down several ideas.**

NOTES:

STEP SIX: Hook

You've come far with this screenwriting book. Congratulations! You should feel proud of your accomplishments. It's hard work, but well worth it. You now understand characters and dialogue and how to craft a story into a screenplay. You have learned how the three acts work into the screenplay. You've been watching movies and reading scripts. We now move on to the story breakdown of the hook and acts, and the actual writing of your screenplay.

First, what does hook mean? It means just that – hook. As a screenwriter you want to hook the audience and reel them into your story. Get the audience involved and make them care about your characters as much as you do. That's why it's so important to really take the time to fully develop characters because you must completely and utterly "love" your characters, even the bad ones. You must know every little aspect of them – even their deepest darkest secrets.

You need to successfully hook or "pique the interest" of the reader/moviegoer and you will leave them wanting more of the story.

They will want to know what happens to the protagonist and wonder how the story will end. The audience must identify with the protagonist in some way, where they can actually see and understand the struggles and conflicts along the journey. Imagine that being a screenwriter means that you are taking the rest of us through a journey of conflicts and struggles.

A hook is an incident or happening that makes the audience interested in the movie. Please remember this doesn't have to be something so enormous like a major 250-car pileup on the Interstate or the end of the world to be defined as the hook. It can be something as simple as a divorce or being fired from a job. But the hook must be the incident that sets the tone and the rest of the screenplay firmly in motion.

Let's take a look at the three movies I've chosen earlier in the book: Moonstruck, The Sixth Sense, and The Matrix. These are three of my favorite movies and most people either have at least heard of them or have seen them more than once. I would suggest renting them if you haven't seen them and refreshing your memory if you have viewed them before.

Please note the following:

A hook needs to take place in the first 5-7 minutes of the movie, which means in the first 5-7 pages of your screenplay. Of course, there are exceptions, but if you stick with this format you are sure to develop a successful screenplay.

Lets take look at Moonstruck and read the first few pages to locate the actual hook. Take a look at how the characters are introduced and how they interact with each other. Only read as far as the hook. We'll get back to the rest of the screenplay later.

http://scifiscripts.com/msol/moonstruck.txt

Yep you've probably guessed it. The hook is where Johnny proposes to Loretta. But I want you to look at all of the characters and events that lead up to the hook. What do we learn about Loretta the protagonist?

- ✓ Italian
- ✓ Dresses sensibly
- ✓ 37 years old
- ✓ Hairstyle is dated
- ✓ She does bookkeeping for local businesses in the neighborhood
- ✓ Tough and efficient
- ✓ Looks out for Johnny

How did the screenwriter craft Loretta's introduction to lead up to the hook?

- ✓ Several scenes of Loretta with interesting business owner characters (see how important all characters are to the screenplay)
- ✓ Through dialogue and action

Then we see Loretta with Johnny in a romantic restaurant drinking red wine. Notice the description of Johnny. We get a great picture in our minds of his character.

For a brief scene, there is a fight between a couple in the restaurant, which acts as a distraction. However, one of these characters will be important later on in the story.

We learn through the dialogue of the Waiter that Johnny is going to propose to Loretta. Nervously through action and dialogue Johnny finally proposes to Loretta. This is the screenplay's hook. It has taken this particular story up a notch and we want to know what's going to happen next.

Take a moment and re-read the scenes leading up to the hook. Study how the screenwriter moves through the scenes, describes characters, and writes short quick dialogue. Everything is important and nothing is frivolous.

Let's look at The Sixth Sense and locate the hook.

http://scifiscripts.com/scripts/sixth-sense.txt

You've guessed it. This one is easier to see. The hook is where a stranger (Vincent) shoots Malcolm the protagonist. What have we learned about Malcolm up to this point?

- ✓ 30 years old
- ✓ Thick wavy hair
- ✓ Striking intelligent eyes

✓ Received an award for outstanding achievement in child psychology

✓ Wife – Anna

✓ Has close relationship with Anna

How did the screenwriter craft Malcolm's introduction to lead up to the hook?

✓ Relationship with Anna

✓ Stranger (Vincent) turned out to be someone that Malcolm worked with when he was ten

✓ Diagnosed Vincent with a mood disorder

✓ Vincent says Malcolm has failed him

✓ Through dialogue and action

Take a moment to look at the scenes leading up to the hook. There's plenty of emotion and suspense packed into these scenes.

Finally, lets look at The Matrix and locate the hook.

http://www.scifiscripts.com/scripts/matrix_96_draft.txt

What's the hook? This screenplay is a little bit different. It starts off with a bang. And I mean a bang! It grips us from the beginning. We're intrigued with Trinity and the computer technology. Not quite sure what we're seeing yet. Is Trinity not from this world? Who really is the bad guy? How did she disappear? So many questions...

The hook is when Trinity escapes from Agent Smith in the phone booth. This is what sets the tone for the rest of the screenplay, even though we haven't met our protagonist yet. This particular scene takes the story up another level. It was a thrill ride from the first page!

Even if you've seen these movies, it's quite different to go back and view them again with the perspective of writing a screenplay. I would suggest reading these three screenplays several times up to the point of the hook only. Don't rush through this Step – take your time. This is an important step that will be implemented into the first draft of your screenplay. Know it well.

I'm sure these screenplays are inspiration for your own screenplay. Begin outlining your screenplay leading up to the hook. Maybe you already have an idea in mind of what your hook is going to be. Really think about how you're going to introduce characters, and how you're going to write dialogue and action. Remember to hook the audience and reel them in…

(Please note that there are different versions of produced screenplays. The written screenplay version may be different from the movie version.)

Quiz #7

1. **Which protagonist character is a child psychologist?**
    a. Malcolm
    b. Loretta
    c. Johnny
    d. Trinity
    e. None of the above

2. **Which character has the most computer technology experience?**
    a. Malcolm
    b. Loretta
    c. Johnny
    d. Trinity
    e. None of the above
    f. All of the above

3. **Which protagonist character is married?**
    a. Malcolm
    b. Loretta
    c. Johnny
    d. Trinity
    e. None of the above
    f. All of the above

4. **Which statement best describes a "hook" in a screenplay?**
    a. the main event of the screenplay
    b. the first few pages of the screenplay
    c. an incident or happening that makes the audience interested in the screenplay
    d. the beginning of the screenplay
    e. None of the above
    f. All of the above

5. **What three movies are referenced in this book for illustration purposes?**
    a. The Matrix, Copycat, Moonstruck
    b. Moonstruck, The Sixth Sense, The Matrix
    c. The Sixth Sense, The Matrix, The Shining
    d. The Matrix, Moonstruck, The Godfather
    e. None of the above
    f. All of the above

6. **What was the hook in The Matrix?**
   a. wedding proposal
   b. shooting
   c. escape in phone booth
   d. fired from job
   e. None of the above

7. **What was the hook in The Sixth Sense?**
   a. wedding proposal
   b. shooting
   c. escape in phone booth
   d. fired from job
   e. None of the above

8. **What was the hook in Moonstruck?**
   a. wedding proposal
   b. shooting
   c. escape in phone booth
   d. fired from job
   e. None of the above

9. **Get the audience involved and make them care about your characters as much as you do.**
   True or False?

10. **The hook must be the incident that sets the rest of the screenplay in place.**
    True or False?

Assignment #6:

✓ **Refer back to your outline for the beginning, middle, and end of your screenplay.**

✓ **Write a paragraph describing each of the scenes in the 1st Act of your screenplay just up to the hook (first 5-7 pages). Write as much detail as possible to convey your scenes without dialogue (for now).**

✓ **Keep in mind your premise, storyline, characters, dialogue, scenes, and hook.**

✓ **Write out your scenes and description up to the hook of your screenplay (no dialogue yet).**

For example:

INT. COFFEE SHOP – DAY
Dick meets Jane. He is infatuated by her beauty and wit.

EXT. PARKING LOT – DAY
Jane confides in Dick and tells him that she's really a stripper.

NOTES:

STEP SEVEN: Set up - 1ˢᵗ Act

This is the most exciting part of the screenplay process. By now you've outlined the beginning, middle, and end of your screenplay. You've developed your characters and dialogue, and you've got your hook. Now you will put the pieces together that will ultimately be the first draft of your screenplay. Hopefully you've spent some time reading and studying the suggested screenplays, and watching your favorite movies. What a great homework assignment watching your favorite movies!

Stop for a moment to review…

If you feel ready and have the above outlines for your screenplay continue with this step. **Stop** right here if you don't feel ready to proceed. I would suggest studying the previous steps a bit more and continue to brainstorm for ideas. You have been bombarded with quite a bit of information and assignments. It's okay to take a breather and reevaluate everything you've learned so far before moving ahead.

But if you're ready... let's go!

The 1st Act consists of the setup to the screenplay. This is where you've introduced characters, established the tone, and hooked the audience. It sounds simple enough. Actually setting up the 1st Act of your screenplay is the most crucial because it integrates the tone and pace for the rest of your story. It's not to say that the 2nd and 3rd Acts aren't important, but the success of your screenplay weighs heavily upon the foundation of the 1st Act. Spend time and attention on this process to set up your screenplay properly.

What happens at the end of the 1st Act? The end of the 1st Act is called Plot Point 1 (PP1). It is defined by the first inciting incident of the 1st plot point to the story. In other words, there must be some type of turning point that moves the screenplay up to the next level.

Remember, PP1 is different from the hook. The hook is there to grab the reader/moviegoer to make them interested in your story. It takes place early on in the screenplay. PP1 is the first turning point in your story that takes place at the end of the 1st Act.

If you don't plan the pacing for your screenplay it will become boring and stale. You must keep raising the stakes for the protagonist and engage the audience. The 1st Act is not a formula but rather a blueprint that keeps the screenplay on track with an entertaining story.

Let's quickly review first:

➢ One page of a screenplay is approximately one minute of screen time.

➢ An average screenplay is anywhere from 90 to 120 pages or 1 ½ to 2 hours.

➢ There are always exceptions with long epic movies or short subject films (you don't need to worry about those types of screenplays now).

➢ Keep your written screenplay on track with no more than 120 pages.

➢ A hook needs to take place in the first 5-7 minutes of the movie, which means in the first 5-7 pages of your screenplay.

➢ If possible, you should have 95 to 110 pages of a tightly written final screenplay.

With all of that being said, how long is the 1st Act? If we are talking about a 120 page script, your PP1, or the ending of the 1st Act should fall somewhere between pages 25-27. The psychology behind a good screenplay is that audiences can become bored and disinterested in a story if there isn't a turning point to up the stakes of the story. This just follows good screenwriting and good action/dialogue skills.

If your PP1 occurs later than page 27, you need to go back to tighten and edit your screenplay. It sounds easy, but it requires planning and rewrites – even from the best screenwriters.

Lets take a look at our three screenplay examples from the previous step. First, let's look at Moonstruck:

http://scifiscripts.com/msol/moonstruck.txt

Johnny must go to Palermo to see his dying mother and he asks Loretta to invite his brother to the wedding. According to Johnny, there's bad blood and they haven't spoken for five years. He wants to make amends with his brother. Loretta visits Ronny in order to invite him to the wedding. We are introduced to Ronny and find out how tormented he is and how he blames his brother for his missing hand.

What is the first turning point of the screenplay? The first turning point would be Johnny going to Palermo to visit his mother so she can give him her blessing for the wedding. At the same time Loretta must invite Johnny's brother to the wedding. These are turning points that bring the story up a notch. Loretta and Johnny can't get married until they have the mother's blessing – end of the 1st Act.

Let's look at The Sixth Sense:

http://scifiscripts.com/scripts/sixth-sense.txt

This story is a little bit different. The 1ˢᵗ Act builds with the two characters of Malcolm and Cole. The 1ˢᵗ Act revolves and continues to build around Cole's condition and the fact that he's absolutely frightened of something. We're not quite sure what it is yet. PP1 is the incident where Cole sees and understands the dead. Take note of the scene at Mr. Marshal's house. Also, take notice of how the dialogue is composed between Malcolm and Cole. This is a very complex screenplay but expertly crafted.

And now, lets look at The Matrix:

http://www.scifiscripts.com/scripts/matrix_96_draft.txt

PP1 is when Neo is at work and receives a cell phone via Federal Express and speaks to Morpheus. Morpheus warns him that "they" are coming for him and that he needs to get out now. The scenes continue with exciting escapes. This indeed takes the screenplay up to the next level and puts the audience on edge. We want to know what he's going to do next.

Again, notice how crisp and concise the dialogue is between Neo, Morpheus, and Trinity. This is quite a bit to digest in writing a screenplay. Spend some time working with your 1ˢᵗ Act. Work it backwards and forwards. Remember you're a screenwriter now!

(Please note that there are different versions of produced screenplays. The written screenplay version may be different from the movie version.)

Quiz #8

1.   **What defines the 1ˢᵗ Act of a screenplay?**
      a. Hook
      b. plot point 1
      c. high-concept
      d. premise
      e. None of the above
      f. All of the above

2.   **_____ is a detailed original idea of the screenplay that has mass audience appeal.**

3.   **One page of a screenplay is approximately one minute of screen time.**
      True or False?

4.   **A logline is still a short one line of 25 words or less that summarizes the screenplay because it brings a more colorful description and detail to the idea.**
      True or False?

5.   **EXT. refers to the interior scene in the screenplay.**
      True or False?

6.   **The 1ˢᵗ Act of the screenplay should fall between 25-27 pages.**
      True or False?

7.   **Creating believable characters in a screenplay is essential.**
      True or False?

8.   **Briefly describe PP1 in Moonstruck.**

9.   **Briefly describe PP1 in The Matrix.**

10. **Briefly describe PP1 in The Sixth Sense.**

Assignment #7:

✓ **Go back to your notes where you wrote a brief outline for the beginning, middle, and end of your screenplay. More than likely, you have revised this several times. Continue to revise .**

✓ **Write a paragraph describing each of the scenes in the 1st Act of your screenplay up to PP1. Write as much detail as possible to convey your scenes without dialogue.**

✓ **Write out your scenes and description up to the 2nd Act of your screenplay.**

For example:

INT. COFFEE SHOP – DAY
Dick meets Jane. He is infatuated by her beauty and wit.

EXT. PARKING LOT – DAY
Jane confides in Dick and tells him that she's really a stripper.

NOTES:

STEP EIGHT: Struggle & Conflict – 2nd Act

You're embarking on the second most important part of the screenplay process and often the most difficult. The 2nd Act of the screenplay is the middle or "meat" of the story. This is where there are confrontations, struggles and conflicts for the protagonist. This is where the skill of the screenwriter takes us through a story gauntlet.

Let's quickly review first. Remember this table on what makes up story?

- ➢ Action and Dialogue = Scenes
- ➢ Scenes = Acts
- ➢ Acts = Beginning + Middle + End
- ➢ Beginning + Middle + End = Story
    - ✓ Story Beginning = 1st Act (set up)
    - ✓ Story Middle = 2nd Act (struggle & conflict)
    - ✓ Story End = 3rd Act (resolution)

1. A **hook** is an incident or happening that makes the audience interested in the movie. A hook needs to take place in the first 5-7 minutes of the movie, which means in the first 5-7 pages of your

screenplay. Of course, there are exceptions but if you stick with this format you are sure to develop a successful screenplay.

2. The 1st **Act** consists of the setup to the screenplay. You've introduced characters, set the tone, and hooked the audience. The setting up the 1st Act of your screenplay is the most crucial because it sets the tone and pace for the rest of your story. A 120 page script, your PP1 or the ending of the 1st Act should fall somewhere between pages 25-27.

Now, you're ready to write the main part of the screenplay with the most pages. This part of the screenplay will be approximately 50 pages.

What happens at the end of the 2nd Act? The end of the 2nd Act is called Plot Point 2 (PP2). It is defined by the second major plot point to the story. This turning point brings the screenplay up to the resolution. This PP2 must be bigger than any other incident – the biggest turning point in the entire screenplay.

How long is the 2nd Act? If we are talking about a 120 page script, your PP2 or the ending of the 2nd Act, should fall somewhere between pages 75-77.

Keep these questions in mind when constructing the 2nd Act.

- Have you built a solid premise?
- Have you outlined all of the scenes?
- Do your characters have depth?
- Do you have a strong hook?

- Have you set up the beginning of the 2nd Act with a solid PP1?

- Are all of your scenes in the 2nd Act absolutely necessary?

- Have you woven sub-plots throughout the 2nd Act?

- Do you need to research any part of your screenplay?

- Does your 2nd Act set up PP2?

For the sake of conformity, let's look at our three previous screenplays.

Here's Moonstruck: http://scifiscripts.com/msol/moonstruck.txt

Loretta gives into Ronny, even though she is engaged to his brother. It's a miracle, Johnny's mother is not going to die and he comes back to tell Loretta he can't marry her. If he marries her, his mother will die.

These are major turning points that bring the screenplay up another notch before the resolution.

However, Loretta our protagonist has raised her stakes in the screenplay. She has now fallen in love with her fiancé's brother. This is the true PP2 in the screenplay.

Let's take a look at The Sixth Sense:

http://scifiscripts.com/scripts/sixth-sense.txt

First, I want to convey that this is really an incredible script from page one. Take some time to study the construction of this particular screenplay.

Cole's performance in his play is a turning point. This is the first time that we actually see him happy and adjusted. His conversation with Malcolm is that there's nothing left to say. Cole decides to open up to his mother and confide in her about how he sees dead people. These scenes are powerful and quite chilling.

Take notice of the dialogue between Malcolm and Cole.

Malcolm says, "I think we've said everything we've needed to say. Maybe it's time to say things to someone else? Someone close to you?"

Also, look at the dialogue between Cole and Lynn.

Cole says, "I'm ready to communicate with you now. Tell you my secrets."

Take note of both of these scenes. They are powerful and great examples of dialogue and scene structure.

Here's The Matrix:

http://www.scifiscripts.com/scripts/matrix_96_draft.txt

This non-stop sci-fi action keeps us on the edge of our seats.

When Neo, Trinity, and Morpheus escape the matrix hotel, Trinity flees in the helicopter. Neo steps in and reveals that he really is "The One".

Notice some of the dialogue even between all of the high-powered action.

Morpheus says, "Do you believe me now? He's the One. Who else could have done this?"

Neo replies, "Morpheus, I know you won't believe me but the Oracle told me I'm not the One."

Notice how the dialogue and PP2 moves into the final resolution. We will study more on the resolution in the next Lesson. For now, just re-read these scenes up to PP2.

There are many things to think about when writing the 2nd Act of the screenplay. It is the "meat" of the screenplay and is extremely important. This is where good notes and outlines play a major part of constructing this section of the screenplay. Take your time and use your notes. Rearrange your notes and index cards many times before settling on your actual scenes. Never stop brainstorming.

Remember, watching all kinds of movies and reading screenplays will only help to enhance your knowledge of how a screenplay is constructed. Try to write every day. This will help keep the creative juices flowing and prevent any "writer's block".

(Please note that there are different versions of produced screenplays. The written screenplay version may be different from the movie version.)

Quiz #9

1. **What makes up action and dialogue?**
   a. plot point 1
   b. plot point 2
   c. scenes
   d. 1st Act
   e. None of the above
   f. All of the above

2. **What defines the 2nd Act of a screenplay?**
   a. Hook
   b. plot point 1
   c. plot point 2
   d. 1st Act
   e. None of the above
   f. All of the above

3. **You should always stay true to your character's dialogue.**
   True or False?

4. **Which of the following is a screenplay genre.**
   a. war historical
   b. action adventure
   c. black comedy
   d. historical drama
   e. All of the above
   f. None of the above

5. **The 2nd Act of the screenplay should fall between 75-77 pages.**
   True or False?

6. **The average screenplay is approximately 120 pages long.**
   True or False?

7. **The 2nd Act is the "meat" of the screenplay and includes the confrontations, struggles, and conflicts of the protagonist.**
   True or False?

8. **Briefly describe PP2 in Moonstruck.**

9. **Briefly describe PP2 in The Matrix.**

10. **Briefly describe PP2 in The Sixth Sense.**

Assignment #8:

✓ **Go back to your notes where you wrote a brief outline for the beginning, middle, and end of your screenplay. More than likely, you have revised this several times.**

✓ **Write a paragraph describing each of the scenes in the 2nd Act of your screenplay up to PP2. Write as much detail as possible to convey your scenes without dialogue (for now).**

✓ **Write out your scenes and description up to the 2nd Act of your screenplay.**

For example:

INT. COFFEE SHOP – DAY
Dick meets Jane. He is infatuated by her beauty and wit.

EXT. PARKING LOT – DAY
Jane confides in Dick and tells him that she's really a stripper.

NOTES:

STEP NINE: Resolution – 3rd Act

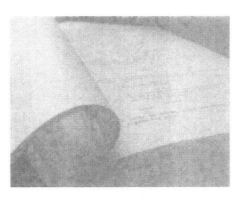

You have now reached the end of your screenplay. It's that part of the movie where audiences can take a deep breath of relief, stand up and cheer, or cry about heartfelt losses. Now you need to wrap up your ending. Sounds easy enough? There are just a few things that you need to keep in mind when you write your 3rd Act.

Let's quickly review three important things to remember before we wrap up the screenplay. This is a screenwriter's "check list" before writing the final resolution.

1. The **hook** is an incident or happening that makes the audience interested in the movie. A hook needs to take place in the first 5-7 minutes of the movie, which means in the first 5-7 pages of your screenplay. Of course, there are exceptions, but if you stick with this format you are sure to develop a successful screenplay.

2. The **1st Act** consists of the setup to the screenplay. You've introduced characters, set the tone, and hooked the audience.

Setting up the 1st Act of your screenplay is the most crucial because it sets the tone and pace for the rest of your story. The end of the 1st Act is called Plot Point 1 (PP1). A 120 page script, your PP1, or the ending of the 1st Act, should fall somewhere between pages 25-27.

3. The **2nd Act** is defined by the second major plot point to the story. This turning point brings the screenplay up to the resolution. The end of the 2nd Act is called Plot Point 2 (PP2). PP2 must be bigger than any other incident – the biggest turning point in the entire screenplay. A 120 page script, your PP2 or the ending of the 2nd Act should fall somewhere between pages 75-77.

You've written most of your screenplay and now it's time for the end. There are a few things to remember when completing your screenplay.

- ✓ Resolve the final conflict of PP2
- ✓ Make the ending final and definite
- ✓ Be sure that you show the protagonist change in some way
- ✓ Answer any outstanding questions in the protagonist's mind
- ✓ Does the resolution make sense?
- ✓ The final resolution can be positive or negative
- ✓ The final scenes of the screenplay should bring the entire story to the forefront
- ✓ The ending should be deliberate
- ✓ The ending should be clear to the audience

The 3rd Act is an important element of the screenplay. If the resolution doesn't make sense, then the entire screenplay doesn't make sense.

If you've taken careful notes and outlined your characters, scenes, and storyline, your screenplay will be in good shape. This is an exciting part of the screenwriting process. You now see the light at the end of the tunnel and your screenplay is finally in a professional format.

You deserve a pat on the back for all of your hard work. Take a moment and celebrate. Many people don't get this far and you deserve all of the credit. Congratulations!

Now, let's look at our three screenplays again and check the 3rd Act against our "check list".

First, let's look at Moonstruck:

http://scifiscripts.com/msol/moonstruck.txt

✓ Resolve the final conflict of PP2

Yes. Mr. Johnny couldn't marry Loretta, because in his mind his mother would die if he did. But Loretta marries Ronny, her true love. Everything worked out for everyone. It was an entertaining story about family and relationships.

✓ Make the ending final and definite

Absolutely.

✓ Be sure that the protagonist changes in some way

Yes, Loretta went from a drab bookkeeper moving throughout her day to a new happier person. She finally came into her own: a new life.

✓ Answer any outstanding questions in the protagonist's mind

Yes, Loretta's inhibitions were realized and she moved on. She met the man of her dreams.

✓ Does the resolution make sense?

Absolutely.

✓ The final resolution can be positive or negative

This ending is positive.

✓ The final scenes of the screenplay should bring the entire story to the forefront.

The final scenes bring the story all the way around from the beginning. The protagonist gets what she wants.

✓ The ending should be deliberate

The ending is deliberate with the marriage of Loretta and Ronny.

✓ The ending should be clear to the audience

Absolutely, the ending is clear.

Here's The Sixth Sense: http://scifiscripts.com/scripts/sixth-sense.txt

✓ Resolve the final conflict of PP2

Yes, Cole now realizes that he can confide in his mother and tell her everything. Malcolm realizes that he is really dead and it's time to move on. This was a very powerful 3rd Act.

✓ Make the ending final and definite

The ending was definite and didn't leave the audience guessing.

✓ Be sure that the protagonist changes in some way

Malcolm changes because he has now helped a young boy to deal with his unique problems and trust.

✓ Answer any outstanding questions in the protagonist's mind

Yes, Malcolm knows he is still a good child psychologist and that his wife loves him.

✓ Does the resolution make sense?

Absolutely.

✓ The final resolution can be positive or negative

This ending is mostly positive. However, it is negative that Malcolm died. But many positive things came out of it.

✓ The final scenes of the screenplay should bring the entire story to the forefront

The final scenes bring around the beginning again with the death of Malcolm.

✓ The ending should be deliberate

Absolutely.

✓ The ending should be clear to the audience

No doubt in the audience's mind.

Finally, The Matrix:

http://www.scifiscripts.com/scripts/matrix_96_draft.txt

✓ Resolve the final conflict of PP2

Yes, Neo defeats Agent Smith after being killed. He is truly the chosen One. He also found his true love with Trinity.

✓ Make the ending final and definite

Yes, the ending is definite. Good overcomes evil. However, it still leaves room for sequels.

✓ Be sure that the protagonist changes in some way

Absolutely, Neo was just an ordinary computer genius and changed into The One in the matrix.

✓ Answer any outstanding questions in the protagonist's mind

Yes, any questions have now been answered. He has a new purpose in life.

✓ Does the resolution make sense?

Absolutely. No questions.

✓ The final resolution can be positive or negative

The ending was positive. It gives a whole new meaning to the endless fight of good versus evil.

✓ The final scenes of the screenplay should bring the entire story to the forefront.

The beginning and ending come full circle. Now there's a new good guy leading the way.

✓ The ending should be deliberate

Absolutely.

✓ The ending should be clear to the audience

No doubt in the audience's mind.

These three screenplays should help to assist you in understanding the importance and the role of all three acts in a screenplay. Remember, screenplays are lean written material to express action and dialogue in order to tell the story. Practice and rewrites will help you to become more efficient in writing such material.

This book presents the screenwriting building blocks that will help you to get to your goal of writing and completing a full-length professional screenplay. Take advantage of all of the lessons, self-check quizzes, assignments, and web links to propel you to your goal of a completed screenplay.

Quiz #10

1. _____ is one line summary of the screenplay.

2. **If the resolution doesn't make sense, then the entire screenplay doesn't make sense.**
   True or False?

3. **What does the 3rd Act accomplish to resolve the story?**
   a. final and definite ending
   b. positive ending
   c. the protagonist should die
   d. confusing the audience
   e. None of the Above
   f. All of the Above

4. **When should you copyright your screenplay?**
   a. When you have finished your screenplay
   b. Before you finish your screenplay
   c. When you've polished your script and before you send it to an agent, production company, or script consultant
   d. Only if you send it to a production company
   e. None of the Above

5. **What is a protagonist?**
   a. The most understanding character in the screenplay.
   b. The most interesting character in the screenplay.
   c. The central character in the screenplay.
   d. The villain character in the screenplay.
   e. None of the above

6. **Which guideline is <u>NOT</u> helpful when writing dialogue?**
   a. stay true to your character's dialogue
   b. keep sentences short and to the point
   c. use action to "show don't tell" instead of dialogue
   d. use monologues only when necessary
   e. None of the above

7. **What three movies were studied in this book?**
   a. The Matrix, Copycat, Moonstruck
   b. Moonstruck, The Sixth Sense, The Matrix
   c. The Sixth Sense, The Matrix, The Shining
   d. The Matrix, Moonstruck, The Godfather
   e. None of the Above
   f. All of the Above

8. Briefly describe the resolution in **Moonstruck**.

9. Briefly describe the resolution in **The Matrix**.

10. Briefly describe the resolution in **The Sixth Sense**.

Assignment #9:

✓ Go back to your notes where you wrote a brief outline for the beginning, middle, and end of your screenplay. More than likely, you have revised this several times.

✓ Write a paragraph describing each of the scenes in the 3rd Act of your screenplay. Write as much detail as possible to convey your scenes without dialogue (for now).

✓ Write out your scenes and description up to the 3rd Act of your screenplay.

For example:

INT. COFFEE SHOP – DAY
Dick meets Jane. He is infatuated by her beauty and wit.

EXT. PARKING LOT – DAY
Jane confides in Dick and tells him that she's really a stripper.

NOTES:

STEP TEN: First Draft of Screenplay

FADE IN:

CONGRATULATIONS!!! You're almost there. Great job! You have just one more important assignment that will tie the entire book together. And it's definitely the most fun!

Let's quickly review. You have the understanding of the following:

- ✓ How to put together a screenwriting work schedule and sticking to it.

- ✓ Premise is what inspires and awakens the creativity of the screenwriter.

- ✓ Logline is still a short one line of 25 words or less that summarizes the screenplay, but it brings a more colorful description and detail.

✓ Screenplay format is the layout of your actual written form.

✓ Copyright protects the written works and the writer as legal proof of originality from fraud and theft.

✓ Writer's Guild of America – West is a form of registering that is intended to register your screenplay as legal evidence and establishes a date for the material's existence.

✓ Characters – protagonist and nemesis.

✓ Dialogue refers to what characters say in the screenplay.

✓ Story is the "main event" of the screenplay.

✓ Hook is an incident or happening that makes the audience interested in the movie.

✓ 1st Act – PP1 is the setup to the screenplay. You've introduced characters, set the tone, and hooked the audience.

- ✓ 2nd Act – PP2 is defined by the second major plot point to the story. This major turning point brings the screenplay up to the resolution.

- ✓ 3rd Act is the resolution and wrap-up of the screenplay.

Let's not forget the following diagram:

- ➢ Action and Dialogue = Scenes
- ➢ Scenes = Acts
- ➢ Acts = Beginning + Middle + End
- ➢ Beginning + Middle + End = Story
  - ✓ Story Beginning = 1st Act (setup)
  - ✓ Story Middle = 2nd Act (struggle & conflict)
  - ✓ Story End = 3rd Act (resolution)

1. The **hook** is an incident or happening that makes the audience interested in the movie. A hook needs to take place in the first 5-7 minutes of the movie, which means in the first 5-7 pages of your screenplay. Of course, there are exceptions, but if you stick with this format you are sure to develop a successful screenplay.

2. The **1st Act** consists of the setup to the screenplay. You've introduced characters, set the tone, and hooked the audience.

Setting up the 1st Act of your screenplay is the most crucial because it sets the tone and pace for the rest of your story. The end of the 1st Act is called Plot Point 1 (PP1). A 120 page script, your PP1 or the ending of the 1st Act should fall somewhere between pages 25-27.

3. The **2nd Act** is defined by the second major plot point to the story. This turning point brings the screenplay up to the resolution. The end of the 2nd Act is called Plot Point 2 (PP2). PP2 must be bigger than any other incident – the biggest turning point in the entire screenplay. A 120 page script, your PP2 or the ending of the 2nd Act should fall somewhere between pages 75-77.

4. The **3rd Act** is the final wrap up. Simply stated, the resolution to your screenplay. In other words, you've written your screenplay and now it's time for the end.

Take a moment to test your understanding of everything you've learned about screenwriting up to this point. Go over your notes, review steps and assignments, and makes notes about any questions you might have.

Screenwriting is a constantly evolving writing process. The best part of doing your screenwriting assignments is that you get to watch movies and read scripts. Get exposure to all kinds of movie genres even if you're only interested in one type of genre. There is much to be learned about screenwriting and there's a tremendous amount of material available.

SCENES

I want to talk a little bit more about the scenes. As you know scenes are made up of action and dialogue. Every scene, whether it's one page or five pages, must have an "action" and a "reaction". Carefully go over your scenes and make absolutely sure that the scene serves a purpose. You have to write lean, and with purpose.

- Ask yourself the following questions when constructing a scene.
- Does the scene serve a specific purpose in the screenplay?
- Does the scene drive the storyline?
- Does the dialogue seem tight and specific?
- Did the scene serve an "action" and "reaction"?
- Does the scene begin and end the same? If so, rewrite or delete the scene.
- Does the scene begin and end on a different tone?

REWRITES

I want to talk a little bit about rewrites. I can't express to you enough that rewrites are a part of the screenwriting process. So you better get used to the idea. Once you think your screenplay is finished. Rewrite. Once you think that your screenplay is good. Rewrite. Once you've completed a rewrite. Rewrite again.

Screenwriting is a wonderful creative process. However, since a screenplay is a tight and concise form of writing, it's more important than ever to make sure it has had enough rewrites. That is not to say that your screenplay isn't good, but there's always room for improvement. Tighten a scene. Give your character a little more depth. Give the storyline a tighter premise. Tie the beginning to the end to properly clarify the story.

Always ask yourself the following questions when rewriting.

- Is there a solid premise?
- Do I absolutely love my story?
- Is it high-concept?
- Is the dialogue tight and lean?
- Are the characters believable?
- Do I absolutely love all of my characters?
- Have I outlined all of my scenes?
- Are all of my scenes necessary?
- Have I outlined all of my acts?
- Is there a strong hook?
- Does the hook fall within the first 5-7 pages?
- Is PP1 strong?
- Does it bring the screenplay to the next level?
- Does the 1st Act fall within 25-27 pages?
- Is PP2 strong?

- Does it bring the screenplay to the next inevitable level?
- Does the 2nd Act fall within 75-77 pages?
- Is my written screenplay within 120 pages?

Keep these format tips for getting started on writing your screenplay first draft.

1. All of these tab settings can be stored in a Macro
2. Turn off justification
3. Create a Header for page numbers that will carry to each page (except page 1)
4. Top and Bottom Margins need to be set to ½ inch (.50")
5. Left Margin 1 inch (1.00")
6. Right Margin ¾ inch (.75")
7. Set Tab Settings:

1"	Margin
1.6"	Direction
2.6"	Dialogue
3.3"	Personal Direction
3.9"	Character Name
5.9"	Transitions
7.2"	Page #

8. Courier 12-point font.
9. 8 ½ x 11 regular white paper

IT'S A WRAP

I can't believe this book has come to an end. I hope that you've enjoyed the screenwriting process. You have one final assignment to complete the first draft of your professional screenplay.

FADE OUT.

THE END

First Draft Assignment #10:

✓ Go back to your revised notes where you wrote a brief outline for your beginning, middle, and end of the screenplay.

✓ Go over your three acts that have written scenes with descriptions.

✓ Go over all of your notes. Complete any questions and research that needs to be accomplished in order to finish your screenplay.

✓ Write out in paragraph format exactly the dialogue you want for each scene in your entire screenplay. This may seem like a lot of work, but it's worth it. <u>Do not continue to the last assignment until this assignment is completed.</u>

✓ Finally, with all of the assignments completed in this book, write the first draft of your screenplay with action and dialogue in complete screenplay format!

NOTES:

Bonus Step: Revision & Editing

Congratulations you've completed the first draft of your screenplay. You deserve to enjoy your accomplishment.

But now what?

It's time to put your screenplay away for some time to gain some distance from your project in order to see it more objectively. I would suggest anywhere from a couple of weeks up to two months. You can take this opportunity to work on another project while your current screenplay simmers on the back burner.

Now that you've been through the entire screenplay building block process, you can use this book for as long as you need to or you can refer to a specific section if you get stuck in your screenwriting process. Either way, this book will serve you well as a reference source.

Rewriting is the key in screenwriting for completing a solid, tight script. However, don't be discouraged by any means because you have accomplished what few screenwriters complete – and that's writing your first draft of your screenplay. Every screenwriter rewrites his or her screenplay, often several times, more accurately ten or twelve times. You better get used to the process. You now need to take a critical look at your screenplay. Make sure that there aren't any typos or grammatical issues with the screenplay. Once that is accomplished and you feel certain that the screenplay is edited properly, take a look at your three acts and break them down.

Answer these important questions:

- Do you absolutely love your screenplay, characters, action, and dialogue?
- Is the story high concept?
- Is there a solid premise?
- Is there a strong hook?
- Are the characters believable?
- Do the characters struggle with conflicts?
- Do the characters evolve one way or another?
- Do you absolutely love ALL of your characters?
- Does PP1 bring your story to the next level?
- Do you have a strong second act?
- Is PP2 strong?
- Is the resolution satisfying and a definite ending?

Take a critical look at your screenplay format, premise, storyline, structure, resolution, characters, and dialogue. The next step is taking each scene one by one and scrutinizing everything from the dialogue, action, direction, length, and importance. Make sure that every scene has an action and reaction. Every scene should have a purpose to your story, something should happen at the end of the scene that makes it clarify something different from the beginning. Each scene needs to be equally important when building a solid screenplay. The dialogue must be lean and crisp with an almost rhythmic pace to the story. Rhythm unifies the story and marks the writer's style. Be objective and even brutal when it comes to rewriting your screenplay.

FAQ

What's the best way to use this book?

The best way to use this book is to learn every concept in each step in order to build a successful screenplay. Take each section slowly and read several times if necessary. Don't jump ahead. This book is designed as screenwriting building blocks to build on each step. Be sure that you fully understand each section before continuing to the next. Take advantage of the self check quizzes and do every assignment. If you miss any question from the quiz be sure to understand why before moving on. You will have a first draft of your screenplay in no time if you do every assignment.

What if I don't have a solid premise or logline to my story?

Don't despair. You may need to read Step 1 many times. Watch several of your favorite movies in the genre that interests you the most. Take some time writing in your journal or notebook and brainstorm your ideas. Write everything down that you can think of about the types of stories you want to write. Before you know it, you'll have a working logline to your screenplay.

How many loglines should I write?

The best rule of thumb is to write as many as you can. Don't write just two or three. Write as many ideas as you possibly can. This will only help you to understand the foundation of a screenplay better and to keep your idea firmly in your mind. Keep your notebook handy. You will have some solid loglines for future screenplays.

When should I copyright?

You should copyright your screenplay when you finish your script. Never send out any treatments or copies of your script until you have acquired the copyright.

Should I copyright the first draft or wait until I have the final draft?

Again, you can copyright your screenplay when you have finalized it. But never send out any treatments or copies of the script until you have the acquired copyright.

What happens when I'm stuck on any of the scenes or acts?

The best way to approach this problem is to go back to the step you were on and read again. It could mean that you're trying to rush your screenplay and you need a break. It helps to step back and take a breather. Continue to write in your journal or notebook. You may want to skip a scene or completely delete it before moving on. Either way, you don't need to force the story. Allow your screenplay to build and progress naturally.

What if I can't get research on a subject pertaining to my screenplay?

The best thing to do is to really decide if this research is important to your screenplay. If it is, then try another source such as what I've listed in Step 5: Story.

What if I have more than one protagonist or nemesis?

For most strong screenplays, there's usually one main protagonist. However, that doesn't mean that your protagonist can't have a sidekick, spouse, or best friend. The nemesis works much the same way. You can have a group, weather condition, or ghosts that are the nemesis in your screenplay and that's perfectly acceptable.

What happens if my screenplay becomes a stalled project?

Don't despair, this can happen to anyone. Sometimes you might not have a firm grasp of your story. You may need to do more research or brainstorm more on your original idea. Sometimes you just need to put the project aside and begin working on another idea from scratch. That's why it's best for you to work with several loglines.

Should I write a treatment?

This is a personal decision based on the requirements of submissions. You need to figure out if you're going to submit your screenplay treatment to various production companies or agents and if they accept just a synopsis, treatment, or the entire screenplay. A further note, it's always a good practice to get into the habit of writing treatment of your screenplays and it puts your entire screenplay firmly in your mind in a just a few pages.

Helpful Resources & References

Books:

The Complete Guide to Standard Script Format
By Judith H. Haag and Hillis R. Cole

Screenwriting
The Art, Craft and Business of Film & Television Writing
By Richard Walter

Story
By Robert McKee

The Screenwriter's Bible:
A Complete Guide to Writing, Formatting, and Selling Your Script
By David Trottier

The Screenwriting Formula
By Rob Tobin

The Whole Picture
Strategies for Screenwriting Success in the New Hollywood
By Richard Walter

Writing a Great Movie:
Key Tools for Successful Screenwriting
By Jeff Kitchen

Copyright & Registration:

Library of Congress
Copyright Office
101 Independence Avenue SE
Washington, DC 20559-6000
(202) 707-3000
http://www.copyright.gov/

Writer's Guild of American (WGA) – West
7000 West Third Street
Los Angeles, CA 90048
(323) 782-4500
http://www.wga.org/

Movie Scripts:

The Internet Movie Script Database
Movie scripts
http://www.imsdb.com/

Movie-Page.com
Movie scripts including rare screenplays
http://www.movie-page.com/movie_scripts.htm

Simply Scripts
Television and movie scripts
http://www.simplyscripts.com/

Online Websites:

Hollywood Creative Directory
http://www.hcdonline.com/
Directories for the entertainment industry

Ink Tip
Matching screenplays with entertainment professionals
http://inktip.com/

Scriptwriter's Network
http://www.scriptwritersnetwork.org/swn/

Screenplay Consultant:

Jennifer Chase, Author & Writer
Script Consultant
Coverage Reports, Critique Evaluation, Promotional Cover Letters
http://jenniferchase.vpweb.com/Services.html

Screenwriting Software:

Dramatica Pro
http://www.screenplay.com/p-13-dramatica-pro.aspx

Final Draft
http://www.finaldraft.com/

Movie Magic Screenwriter 6
http://www.screenplay.com/p-29-movie-magic-screenwriter-6.aspx

ScriptBuddy
Online Screenwriting Software
http://www.scriptbuddy.com/

Scriptware
http://www.scriptware.com/

Glossary of Terms

Action
The scene description, character movement, and sound described in a screenplay.

Beat
It refers to an interruption in dialogue. It suggests that the character (actor) should pause a moment before continuing the dialogue.

b.g. (background)
This term is used to describe an action in the background when the attention is focused on the foreground.

Character
The name of the character appears in ALL CAPS when the character is first introduced in the "Action". The character is then written in normal letters in the action and the rest of screenplay.

CLOSE ON
It refers to a camera shot description that suggests a close-up on a person, action, or object.

CONTINUOUS
It refers to an action that moves from one location to another without interruptions of time.

Coverage
This refers to the 3-5 page report that evaluates the potential of a screenplay. This report will recommend, consider, or pass on the screenplay project.

Copyright
This process protects the written works and the writer as legal proof of originality from fraud and theft. (See copyright information above in Step 2: Format)

Cross-Genre

Refers to two mixed genres (see genre). For example, action/adventure, historical/drama, and horror/comedy are cross-genres.

CUT TO:

This refers to a simple transition of scene, character changes, or frame change.

Development

This is the process when a screenplay is developed into a shooting script.

Dialogue

This refers to what characters say in the screenplay.

Direction

This refers to the description of the action in a screenplay.

DISSOLVE TO:

Another common transition, when one scene fades out and another comes into view – also see FADE TO:

EXT.

This simply means exterior. This particular scene takes place outdoors.

FADE TO:

See DISSOLVE TO:

FADE IN:

This refers to the beginning of a screenplay.

FADE OUT.

This refers to the end of the screenplay.

Genre

Refers to the type or variety of the screenplay, for example, comedy, sci-fi, action, and drama are a type of genre.

High-Concept
This refers to an original story that has mass audience appeal. For example, high-concept is a blockbuster commercial screenplay.

Hook
This refers to an incident or happening that makes the audience interested in the movie.

INSERT
This refers to a closeup of an important detail in the screenplay.

INT.
This simply means interior. This particular scene takes place indoors.

Logline
This refers to a one-line summary of the plot and can be 25 words or less describing the screenplay.

Option
This refers to a producer who pays for the rights of the screenplay in a specified period of time.

O.S. (off screen)
This refers to a character's dialogue heard but not seen on the screen.

Personal Direction
This refers to the character's specific direction. For example, sighing, laughing, or yelling are personal directions.

POV
This simply means point of view. It is where we see through someone else's eyes.

Premise
This refers to the foundation or principle idea of the storyline.

Query Letter

This refers to a short letter pitching a professional company in hopes that they will request to read your screenplay.

Scene

This refers to an event that takes place in one location or time.

Spec Script

This refers to a written screenplay that is intended to be sold on the open market but not by a studio or production company. The only way for a new screenwriter to break into the business is to have a strong spec script.

Treatment

This refers to the plot of a screenplay written in one to two pages. The treatment should include the entire, well-written story, with a beginning, middle, and end.

V.O. (voice over)

This refers to a character's voice heard either prior to seeing them or as a narration of a specific event.

Quiz Answers

Quiz #1
1. index cards, binder, notebook, journal, composition book. etc.
2. writing the first draft of your screenplay
3. type or variety of the screenplay
4. 3
5. several times or until you understand the concept discussed
6. yes
7. take each section and work through slowly until you completely understand the concepts.
8. action and dialogue
9. determination, love for writing, etc.
10. Quentin Tarantino, Robert Altman, Leslie Dixon, Ed Solomon, etc.

Quiz #2
1. e
2. High Concept
3. Premise
4. Logline
5. True
6. d
7. e
8. f
9. False
10. True

Quiz #3
1. c
2. b
3. d
4. a
5. b
6. True
7. True
8. False
9. False
10. b

Quiz #4
1. e
2. True
3. False
4. False
5. True

6.   b
7.   False
8.   c
9.   True
10.   c

Quiz #5
1.   a
2.   d
3.   True
4.   False
5.   False
6.   e
7.   f
8.   True
9.   True
10.   False

Quiz #6
1.   A scene or story event is made up of action and dialogue.
2.   Story is the main event of the screenplay.
3.   Action refers to the description of what is happening in the scene.
4.   Dialogue refers to the conversation between characters.
5.   1 screenplay page is approximately 1 minute of screen time.
6.   An act is made up of scenes.
7.   There are three acts in a screenplay.
8.   The 1st act is the beginning of your screenplay.
9.   The 2nd act is the middle of your screenplay.
10.   The 3rd act is the end or resolution of your screenplay.

Quiz #7
1.   a
2.   d
3.   a
4.   c
5.   b
6.   c
7.   b
8.   a
9.   True
10.   True

Quiz #8
1.   b
2.   High Concept

3. True
4. True
5. False
6. True
7. True
8. Johnny must go to Palermo to see his dying mother and he asks Loretta to invite his brother to the wedding.
9. Neo is at work and receives a cell phone via Federal Express and speaks to Morpheus.
10. The incident where Cole sees and understands the dead.

Quiz #9
1. c
2. c
3. True
4. e
5. True
6. True
7. True
8. Loretta gives into Ronny, even though she is engaged to his brother. It's a miracle, Johnny's mother is not going to die and he comes back to tell Loretta he can't marry her. If he marries her, his mother will die.
9. When Neo, Trinity, and Morpheus escape the matrix hotel, Trinity flees in the helicopter. Neo steps in and reveals that he really is "The One".
10. Cole's performance in his play is a turning point. This is the first time that we actually see him happy and adjusted. His conversation with Malcolm is that there's nothing left to say.

Quiz #10
1. Logline
2. True
3. a
4. c
5. c
6. e
7. b
8. Loretta stays with Ronny. Johnny knows that he can't marry Loretta.
9. Neo overcomes the "bad guys" and continues with his destiny.
10. Cole makes peace with his ability to see dead people and decides to tell his mother everything. Malcolm realizes that he is dead, and is also able to help Cole.

About the Author

Jennifer Chase has taught beginning screenwriting for more than two years in the online environment. She has more than ten screenplays to her credit in the suspense, comedy, and drama genres. She currently assists clients with copyrighting, ghostwriting, book reviews, editing, research, and script consulting.

Jennifer holds a bachelor degree in police forensics, master's degree in criminology, and is an affiliate member of the Academy of Behavioral Profiling. She has written and published crime fiction novels: Compulsion, Award Winning Dead Game, and Silent Partner (based on her screenplay).

For more information about Jennifer Chase, please visit:

http://jenniferchase.vpweb.com/

http://authorjenniferchase.blogspot.com/

CPSIA information can be obtained at www.ICGtesting.com
Printed in the USA
LVOW05s1402180614

390639LV00010B/99/P